LOST BODY

LOST BODY
(CORPS PERDU)

BY AIMÉ CÉSAIRE

ILLUSTRATIONS BY
PABLO PICASSO

Introduction and Translation by
CLAYTON ESHLEMAN and ANNETTE SMITH

GEORGE BRAZILLER, INC.   NEW YORK

Published in 1986 by George Braziller, Inc.

Corps Perdu by Pablo Picasso ©1986 by the Estate of Pablo Picasso
V.A.G.A., New York/S.P.A.D.E.M., Paris

Introduction ©1986 by George Braziller

Text by Aimé Césaire translated from the French by Clayton Eshleman
and Annette Smith.
English translation ©1983 by The Regents of the University of California.

Grateful acknowledgement is made to Editions du Seuil for permission to
reprint *Corps Perdu*.

For information address the publisher:

George Braziller, Inc.
One Park Avenue
New York, New York 10016

Library of Congress Cataloguing in Publication Data:

Césaire, Aimé.
  Lost body.

  Translation of: Corps perdu.
  1. Césaire. Aimé—Translations, English.
I. Title.
PQ3949.C44C613 1986   841   86-1001
ISBN 0-8076-1147-6
ISBN 0-8076-1148-4 (pbk.)

Printed in the United States of America

First Printing

CONTENTS

INTRODUCTION

In the summer of 1982, Aimé Césaire granted us an interview in his Paris apartment. On the agenda: the clarification of a short list of words that still puzzled us as we translated *The Complete Poetry*.[1] Césaire's apartment, located in a nondescript part of the city, is small and modestly appointed: a round table covered with an oil cloth, a narrow sofa, a few African masks, at least two beautiful paintings by Wifredo Lam, many books. Césaire answered our questions softly, patiently and eruditely. When the conversation focused on a word that had escaped all our attempts at identification, he did something that seemed to speak volumes about the man. Without hesitation, he took from a shelf a thin, well-worn book (which turned out to be a lexicon of rare and exotic words used in equatorial Africa) and immediately pointed in it at the object of our query—or rather at the word stem from which he had coined the mysterious noun in question. Obviously, this man, seemingly ageless, in a conservative dark suit, who had such an awesome amount of information at his fingertips and who took such liberties with it, was not just another *professeur de lycée*. We were, indeed, in the presence of one of the greatest living poets, as well as the main proponent and exponent of the negritude movement, a veteran statesman, a high-ranking official and a revered figure in the Third World.

Detailed biographies and bibliographies of Aimé Césaire are not lacking,[2] but let us just briefly review his life, which in itself is a paradigm of the destiny of the black people in our era. Born in Basse-Pointe, a small town on the northeast coast of Martinique, into a poor family in 1913, Césaire received a solid secondary education. His good grades propelled him to Paris, where in 1931 he began to prepare for entrance into the prestigious Ecole Normale Supérieure. He stopped his studies short of the *agrégation*, but with his friends Léon Damas, Léopold Senghor and other young intellectuals from the West Indies and Africa, he founded a small newspaper, L'*Etudiant noir*. Through Mademoiselle Nardal's literary *salons* and review he was also in touch with black Americans of the Harlem Renaissance group—Jean Toomer, Langston Hughes, Countee Cullen—and a Jamaican, Claude McKay, whose novel *Banjo*, one of the earliest expressions of the worth of black "primitivism," did not remain unnoticed by Césaire. In 1935, Césaire took a trip to Yugoslavia, where he began writing his *Notebook of a Return to the Native Land* (*Cahier d'un retour au pays natal*), the title anticipating by one year an actual visit to Martinique. But it was only in 1939, after his marriage to Susanne Roussy (in 1937) and the publication of the first version of the *Notebook* in the Parisian review *Volontés*, that Césaire returned to his native country for good.

The *Notebook*[3] is the most famous of Césaire's poetic works. It is a lyrical document that sums up the reckoning of black people first with their blackness and their servitude and then, little by little, with their greatness: their stoicism, their special bonds with nature, the value of their African roots—in brief, their negritude, a word that appeared in print for the first time in this work. The long, vehement 1,055-line narrative goes from sprawling despair inspired by the misery and torpor of the island, through a painful crescendo, to a triumphant upsurge in which the black narrator, now fully aware of his worth, embraces the universe from the helm of a prophetic ship.

As traumatic as his return to Martinique was, it may have been a good thing for Césaire's career. In Martinique, isolated from metropolitan France, Césaire had plenty of time to read and meditate, most particularly on Nietzsche and on the German anthropologist Leo Frobenius's history of African Civilization. In collaboration with his wife, René Ménil, and others, he founded an avant-garde review, *Tropiques*,[4] whose 14 issues (1941–1945) gave him a forum from which to develop his poetics, removed from the French models that had nourished his youth: Lautréamont, Baudelaire, Rimbaud, Mallarmé, Apollinaire. Césaire, who had already been influenced by Surrealism while in France, had an "extraordinary meeting" with Breton in 1941 in Fort-de-France. He was conscious of the subversive potential that Surrealism represented for someone determined to sabotage the French language from the inside. But he was haunted by the plight of the Martinican people and was passionately attached to their land of inescapable natural beauty. In the end, therefore, the systematic otherworldliness of Surrealism did not win him over; instead he harnessed surrealistic techniques to the cause of negritude.

In a way, the conjunction with Surrealism had been a test of Césaire's ideological commitment. *The Miraculous Weapons* (*Les armes miraculeuses*,[5] 1946) is still clearly surrealistic, although it alludes from time to time to World War II and to some heroic itinerary explicit in the lyrical coda to the volume *And the Dogs Were Silent.* However, *Solar Throat Slashed* (*Soleil cou coupé*,[6] 1948) is more evenly divided between entirely personal pieces written in the surrealist style and poems more historically anchored, as evidenced by several poems of African inspiration ("Ex-Voto for a Shipwreck," "All the Way from Akkad from Elam, from Sumer," "To Africa") and by the presence of black Americans on the scene. The conflicting demands of modernism (or "disengaged" poetry) and of a commitment to negritude are perhaps reflected in the theme of dismemberment in a poem like "The Lay of Errantry" in *Lost Body* (*Corps perdu*,[7] 1950), which we will consider more specifically below.

In the meantime (1944), Césaire had paid a lengthy visit to Haiti, homeland of Toussaint l'Ouverture and Henri Christophe, whose example reinforced his political faith. By something of a fluke, Césaire ran as a Communist candidate in the 1945 Fort-de-France municipal elections and, much to most people's (not the least his own) surprise, was elected mayor. Shortly afterward, in October 1945, he became Martinique's deputy to the first French National Assembly. Like the narrator on the symbolic ship of the *Notebook*, Césaire had now to navigate at the helm of his island. Ever since, his long political career has been noted in metropolitan France for its passionate interventions on behalf of the French Antilles and the French colonies in general, and in Martinique for the truly democratic style of his mayoralty. His *Commemoration of the Centennial of the Abolition of Slavery*[8] (1948) and *Discourse on Colonialism*[9] (1950) were solemn warnings to imperialistic powers. Yet he was no one's puppet, and because his concerns were the pragamatic ones of a statesman, he broke away from the Communist party, which, like many a French patriot, he had joined during the war. His *Letter to Maurice Thorez*[10] (1956) finds Communist ideology, at least the European brand, irrelevant to underdeveloped countries and somewhat indifferent to their problems. He found spiritual allies in the editors of and contributors to a new Parisian journal and publishing house dedicated to the Third World, *Présence africaine*, founded by Alioune Diop and others in 1947.

The years of rupture with his former party seem to have been a period of readjustment of his goals and priorities. After *Lost Body*, it took ten years for Césaire to bring out his next collection, *Ferraments* (*Ferrements*,[11] 1960), which, to a greater extent than the earlier volumes, is preoccupied with the past and the future of the black world. The fight for autonomy in African countries and social justice in the Caribbean and the United States inspired a number of poems, while others are somber and fantastic evocations of black bondage throughout history. Still others, less topically related to the ideology, seem to come from a leader already distanced from his cause, although not discouraged.

Another indication of Césaire's shift of priorities is the increasing proportion of drama (a medium with a wider appeal) in his output. *La Tragédie du Roi Christophe* (1963), *Une Saison au Congo* (1967) and *Une Tempête*[12] (1969) deal with colonialism, liberation and the problems of political power from an increasingly mediated point of view.

The last of these plays explores the complex relationship between the colonizer and the colonized under the guise of a free rewriting of Shakespeare's *The Tempest*.

In 1976, Césaire's *Complete Works* were collected in a three-volume edition edited by his son Jean-Paul (Fort-de-France: Editions Désormeaux). Volume I (*Poetry*) includes, under the title *Noria*, a diverse collection of poems, many going back to the 1960s. They continue the more topical vein of *Ferraments* and reflect Césaire's relationship with the Third World ("Letter from Bahia-of-All-Souls" and "Ethopia"), with other artists ("Wifredo Lam"), and with poets (St. John Perse), although not always in full agreement, as in the case of the Haitian Depestre, whom he found too obedient to the Communist party's literary dicta ("The Verb 'Marronner'"). The elegiac note is also represented in the collection. In 1982, he published still another volume, *Moi Laminaire*,[13] a reminder to anyone who is tempted to consider that Césaire's career as a poet is finished.

His political career, although not to everyone's taste, remains equally active. As the leader of the Martinican Progressive party since 1958, and as the frequently re-elected mayor, Césaire succeeded in improving the Martinicans' lot and in generating a considerable cultural renaissance through the SERMAC (Service Municipal d'Action Culturelle). But his struggle to change the status of the island from a colony to a department resulted in questionable benefits that more radical blacks (such as the writer Edouard Glissant) have challenged.[14] Under the Mitterand regime, Césaire has been, since 1981, a member of the majority, all the more reason for younger black militants throughout the world to attack his definition of negritude —or even the notion itself—as outdated. Still, he is periodically mentioned as a strong contender for the Nobel Prize for Literature. As deserved and proper as such an award would be, one could justly consider the Nobel Peace Prize an even more appropriate recognition. In transcending the tragic circumstance of blacks in a constructive way, in channeling violence through a superb poetic *oeuvre*, in giving voice not only to Martinicans but to all blacks, in extending his hand "to all the wounded hands/in the world,"[15] Césaire remains a symbol and a model for all people of good will. Writers on four continents claim him as their own.[16] He represents a true synthesis between the white and the black worlds—the best of both. In this sense he is everyone's patrimony. Those who, whether as Caribbeans, as Africanists, as blacks, as poets, as scholars, as politicians, might want to annex him, can take pride in their defeat.

◆　◆　◆

The ten poems of Lost Body thematically interlock in a fugal manner—in fact, their unity of style and tonal similarity make them read like sections of a single "serial poem." Unlike his first three collections, all of which underwent radical revision, Lost Body has seen only minimal changes. Probably composed at the end of the 1940s, while Césaire was dividing his time between Fort-de-France and Paris, this collection—or suite—offers the reader a rare opportunity to observe the transitional moment in Aimé Césaire's poetry when his youthful Mercurial fervor is being modified and weighted with the elegaic introspection of maturity.

In coining the word negritude, Césaire built an ideological structure in which the négre ("nigger") could find not only refuge but the rafters and supports of a cultural continuity. In Notebook of a Return to the Native Land, Césaire argues that the absence of black achievement is compensated for by an earthy, mystical quality that "yields, captivated, to the essence of things." According to the poet, the fact that blacks have not (in the Western sense) invented or explored and have remained "ignorant of surfaces" implies a potential to regenerate an earth that has (and here we are paraphrasing Césaire) become weary with the victories that become the defeats, alibis and stumblings of the white world. By the time he wrote Lost Body, Césaire seems to have realized that in certain ways the black would remain in exile from himself and, in effect, not enter the house called negritude that Césaire had built for him. The dynamics underlying this somber revisioning are social as well as psychological.

As a mayor and a deputy to the French National Assembly, Césaire was confronting the initial problems involved in improving the lives of his black constituents. Perhaps as a result of this, the speaker in "Who Then, Who Then..." repeatedly expresses the need for assistance in fulfilling various desires—a clearly more social gesture than is expressed in Césaire's earlier poetry ("The Thoroughbreds," for example), in which the speaker destroys and re-creates his world by himself. In general, the early fusillades of revolutionary optimism are now giving way to the difficulties of true change. As several poems movingly testify, the tragic roots of being black in a world governed for the most part by whites are deeper and more embedded than the poet of the *Notebook* had calculated.

Psychologically, in *Lost Body* Césaire is struggling with the erosion of his heroic, fiery, and phallic aspects, with the challenge of time, distance, and the instability of Eros, as well as with an anguished Saturnian suspicion that his condition cannot be explained by colonialism but is somehow a part of nature itself. While mythological forces are still heroically evoked, they are increasingly battered by the myth-denying present. In both the first and the title poem of *Lost Body*, the word "nigger" limits and severely infects mythological amplification. In "Word," the speaker commands the "word" (which initially in the poem suggests the Word, or Logos) to keep vibrating within him. At the moment that its waves lasso and rope him to a vodun center-stake where a shamanic sacrifice ensues, it is also revealed that the "word" is "nigger"—and, by implication, the curare on the arrow tips—as the quiver of social stigmata associated with "the word 'nigger' " are emptied into him.

And in "Lost Body," the speaker is dissolved and reborn in a predictable Césairean fashion, this time as Omphale—a seer Pythoness who in Greek myth guards the Delphic *omphalos*. However, as this seer seeks contact with the wind, he/she receives not a vision but screams of "nigger nigger nigger from the depths/of the timeless sky."

The requests in "Who Then, Who Then..." are responded to at last by a "full-grown girl," who separates the grain of the speaker's shadow from the grains of his clarity while "neatly confusing the accounts." She is to bring into relief Césaire's negative side, until now obscured by his intellectual clarity. Ultimately, then, the speaker's "need" is for more attention to the soul and its grim politicized vales, in contrast to the spirit's soaring peaks. The brooding, meandering lines of this poem show us how far we have come from the climax of the *Notebook*, where a standing insurrection of slaves wheels the poem up into the stars.

The "full-grown girl" of "Who Then, Who Then..." is the first appearance in *Lost Body* of a shadowy feminine presence that evokes both Isis (gathering the scattered pieces of the "lost body" of Osiris) and perhaps an actual woman. The weight of this presence, however, is linked to the fauna and flora of Martinique, as a kind of spirit of the place, increasingly associated with destruction and remorse. In "Elegy," an entropic landscape is paired with a male lover's anguish —for he has discovered that under the surface is not merely, as in the *Notebook*, "a wallow of boars/ ... your eyes which are a shimmering conglomerate of coccinella," but "the herd of old sufferings" that push their way out of the unconscious like dumb, driven beasts, right into the lovers' embrace and turn it into "DISASTER." Here again, one might recall a passage in the *Notebook*, where Césaire describes the "unexpected sorcery" that would lull his father into "melancholy tenderness or drive to towering flames of anger." This "gnawing persistent ache" now seems to be acknowledged by the poet as a negative force in his own life, as if there are aspects of black anguish that cannot be dispelled by Eros or by imagination.

A sense of abrupt violence permeates *Lost Body*. In "Forloining," a few lines from a folk song describing a cane cutter hacking apart the body of a "long-haired [white?] lady" interrupt the poet's plaintive

xiv

meditation on his "Distant . . . inattentive-one." And in "Lost Body," the startling "nigger" screams of the wind inform the speaker that there is madness at the center of his existence. If the wind itself calls him a nigger, then he *is* an eternal fugitive. For a moment, Césaire's body of work buckles with the dilemma that true humanity might only be discovered in madness or apocalypse. The severity of this moment is registered by the wrenching ending where the nigger, although rent apart (by the white devil's hounds), destroys the sky and re-creates primal islands in one paroxysmic gesture. Such an ending recalls Hart Crane's great lyric, "Lachrymae Christi," in which a Nazarene/Dionysus who is crucified, torn asunder and burned at the stake is beseeched to reappear whole. Both poems confront the reader with a radical vision of creativity that is bound up with an assimilation of such destructiveness as to render it, in the same moment, sublime and absurd.

"Your Portrait" continues this work of desperate metamorphosis; here the feminine presence is depicted as a river that carries along the speaker, who envisions himself as the uprooted trunk of a poisonous manchineel. As if desiring to lose this aspect of his body in the feminine element, the speaker prays to become liquid himself. In the following poem, "Summons," enrapt with his liquid transformation, Césaire portrays the earth as a wild and beautiful event, once again erotic, and now liberated by time. The poem ends abruptly with three definitive adjectives stacked against the left margin, one after the other. "whole/native/solemn." Not only has the "lost body" again been recovered, but these words stand as a summation of Césaire's own personality in his work.

This is the self-assertive peak of *Lost Body*. The last two poems are melancholy, meandering streams of images, anticipating many of the poems in Césaire's last major collection, *Ferraments* (1960), in which evocations of a timeless black "diaspora" ring even further changes on the "lost body" theme: the lost collective body as well as the individual body, cast overboard from the slave ships and lost at sea.

In "Lay of Errantry," it is as if the liquid transformation sought in "Your Portrait" has become a style of writing. The sliding, unpunctuated phrase-pulses are riverine in that they collect and carry along countless historical and mythological particles. Here, the peristaltic negations and affirmations of *Lost Body* relax in a flow, at once mournful, questioning, self-defining, and noble. The poem and collection end with the speaker having re-entered Paradise with the flame from the Covering Cherub's flaming sword. The work now, Césaire suggests, is in felling the trees of the Christian Eden, using the gate-guardian's sword flame as an axe. Given the phallic associations with tree shafts that pervade Césaire's poetry at large, the final image resounds with atavistic suffering, experienced as self-maiming at the core of a reconstruction of Paradise.

◆   ◆   ◆

Césaire's interest in Picasso went back at least a decade before the appearance of the 1950 Fragrance edition *of Corps perdu*, for which the illustrations in this book were originally conceived. Articles in *Tropiques*, although not all from his pen, reflect an editorial desire to raise the level of artistic consciousness among the Martinicans and give some clue as to how Picasso's painting intersected with a new definition of art in the framework of negritude. Reviewing M. Alain Couturier's "excellent pages on Picasso," *Tropiques* 4[17] wrote: "One must understand that cubism [is] . . . an art which creates pure objects, devoid of any reference to outside reality. Picasso's genius demonstrated that such objects can be very beautiful and very moving." In addition, Picasso is credited with "creating beauty with the most paradoxical elements, with whatever novelty ugliness and madness and all the nightmares of abomination can summon up. . . . His latest works are awesome." Symetrically, *Tropiques* 6–7[18] explores "the problem of art in Martinique": the artistic inertia of the islanders owed to the conflict in them between a European esthetic ruled by realism and an African esthetic ruled by mysticism. In this paralysis, "Africa has avenged herself." True Martinican art must therefore depart from European models. This preoccupation was indirectly pursued in the same issue of *Tropiques* in a note regarding Picasso's and Wifredo Lam's close friendship. The latter was seen as an example of an artist aware of his African and Caribbean heritage, the former a "prophetic witness of the convulsions of a world." Finally, *Tropiques* 13–14[19] contains a long article by Pierre Loeb on "Painting and Our Times," in which Picasso is praised for a concreteness so extreme that, for him, art amounts to a "gesture." "Picasso," the article continues, "seems destined to find a universal form and esthetic ground. Each one of his gestures takes a historical significance, in a Europe where everything is in ruins." Further, Loeb adds that even more than Matisse, Bonnard and Rouault, it is Picasso who "has espoused his times," who "ahead of all others embraces the universe."

Because Editions Fragrance no longer exists, few details are available on the specific circumstances surrounding the coming together of Picasso and Césaire. All we have been able to establish is that this was not Césaire's initiative. But they were bound to cross paths in the postwar Parisian intellectual circles in which both moved. For instance, each wrote a piece in the pamphlet *Why I Am a Communist*, published by the French Communist party in 1946. In August 1948, Césaire and Picasso both participated in the *Congress of Wroclaw*, a world gathering of intellectuals in favor of peace, organized by a Franco-Polish committee. Both were also among 370 participants who signed an anticolonialist manifesto. In April 1949, both again attended a "meeting of French intellectuals in the defense of peace," during which Césaire read a poem written for the occasion, which may have set off a spark of appreciation between them. Finally, Wifredo Lam, who was a friend both of Césaire and Picasso and who had a joint exhibit with the latter at the Galerie Pierre in 1939, may have been a point of contact, if not a go-between.

Editions Fragrance were not, however, breaking new ground. The collaboration of modern poetry and modern painting—especially Cubism—in book production already was a long-established tradition. In the tumultuous years before and after World War I—which saw Symbolism survive itself, Cubism progagate outside of the bateau-lavoir, Dada bloom and wither, Surrealism and several other "isms" be born—painters and poets intersected with an intimacy unmatched since. As early as 1912, Apollinaire remarked that "most cubist painters live in the company of poets. As for Picasso, who invented new painting and is, undoubtedly, the highest artistic figure of our times, he lived solely among poets of whom I am proud to be one."[20] It was, in a way, the continuation of the "Banquet Years" of the previous generation, so felicitously re-created by Roger Shattuck, but in the postwar years, bars, cafés, and often-scandalous exhibits, manifestos and reviews replaced the banquets. Between 1917 and 1947, painters and poets jointly started no fewer than nineteen small reviews, many of which were extinct after their first number.

In July 1916, Apollinaire presented a reading by Max Jacob, Pierre Reverdy and other poets in front of Picasso's notorious *Demoiselles d'Avignon*. The same year the Lyre and Palette gallery, which exhibited Matisse and Picasso, held a lecture on Max Jacob. In 1917, Jacob himself introduced Reverdy's poems in front of works by Juan Gris and André Lhote. His collection, *Le Cornet à dés* (1917) included such titles as "Poèmes sans forme avec consistance molle" and "Poème en forme de demi-lune," reminiscent of Satie's earlier *Trois morceaux en forme de poire*. Those titles, however, were not meant ironically as Satie's had been, but as a serious proposition: that poetry could be structured in space like an object. This same concern presided over the production of many books.

In 1911, Apollinaire had established a paradigm of such collaborations when he conceived the typography and composition of his *Bestiaire ou Cortège d'Orphée* to mesh with the corresponding illustrations by Dufy. The illustrations were to be a complement to the text, but not enslaved by it, and were to demonstrate the elective affinities between different modes of expression. Blaise Cendrars's *Prose du Transsibérien* (1913) illustrated by Sonia Delaunay and advertised as "the first simultaneous book," Apollinaire's own *Calligrammes* (1913–1918), his *Enchanteur pourrissant* (1908) with woodcuts by Derain, Eluard illustrated by Ernst, Reverdy by Juan Gris—these are but a few landmarks in the history of the interpenetration of words and pictures during the years preceding and following World War I. Picasso himself made a frontispiece for Jacob's *Cornet à dés* (1917) and for Aragon's *Feu de Joie* (1919) and illustrated Ovid's *Metamorphoses* in 1930 and, closer to the Fragrance project, Reverdy's *Chants des morts* in 1948.

Such experiments prompted the hostile critic Fréderic Lefèvre to exclaim that "the prose poem gave up pleasing for being. It has become something like a cubist painting".[21] His quip contributed to the development of the phrase "literary cubism," which was no sooner coined than it was deemed oxymoronic. In the long run, critics and artists agreed that one must talk not of influence but merely of cultural conjunctions and, in Eluard's words, that "in order to collaborate, painters and poets need see themselves as free.... In the end, nothing is as beautiful as an involuntary resemblance."[22] In the case of Césaire and Picasso, their involuntary but significant similarity is what will occupy us here, rather than Picasso's "Surrealism" or Césaire's "Cubism."

Picasso, as the leader of the artistic avant-garde, and Césaire, on two grounds—as influenced by the Surrealists and as one of the figureheads of the négritude movement—both sought a cultural revolution that would transcend the mere renewal of forms. Picasso used to say, "When one works, one must always be against. Never for."[23] He went so far as to demand that "we must kill modern art, " the kind that was no longer modern, or that "a dictatorship of painters" be instituted to eliminate "cheats, habits, charm, history."[24] The fiery *Tropiques* team referred to "charm" as *"littérature doudou,"*[25] and with a metaphor more appropriate to his environment than that of a dictatorship, Césaire compared this escape from traditional Western esthetics to the escape of black slaves ("négres marrons") from their white masters. The words *marrons* (meaning "slaves on the run") and *marronner* (the corresponding verb) are recurrent metaphors by which he designates his poetics and the task of black writers in general. He saw poetry as "insurrectional," "hell-bound," a heritage "of fevers, of seisms."[26] In his case and in Picasso's, revolution meant liberation. Picasso freed the object from the illusions of the senses, the hazard of spatial contingency, the fetters of utilitarianism, the conventions of representation. Césaire loosened it from the deceptive arrangements of logic, from its fixed relationship to linguistic signs. Thus objects were unharnessed, returned to nature to what Breton called "the wild state," before being reconstructed in the dynamic (etymologically speaking, "poetic") unity of the artist's world.

Césaire sought deconstruction as passionately as Picasso and with the same results—what might paradoxically be called a radical realism. For as Picasso forces the viewer to know a guitar, a human nose or a bottle, not as one sees it but as it is made, so Césaire puts his reader amidst "the shivering spawn of forms liberating themselves from facile bondages/and escaping from too premature combinings."[27] From ground zero, the painter and poet then provoke novel relationships among objects by manipulating the pictorial or linguistic signs—in manipulation that does not exclude humor, parody, puns and that taps the Promethean as well as the playful urge in us. Whether these relationships were there all along "in the gnarled, primitive unity of the world"[28] or exist only in this, so to speak, collage of cosmic ambition is a transcendental question whose answer rests on one's personal response to the beauty or the horror of nothingness. Granted such creations sometimes take place in violence, generate outrage, and beget an occasional monster. But are they not monsters only in the eyes of people who confuse sign and sense? Nevertheless, this common gravitational pull to the core of matter makes Picasso and Césaire magnificently *concrete*—a quality one sees in their commitment to life, therefore to politics. In the name of purity, neither gave in to systems. Picasso did not disdain to put Cubism in the service of peace, nor did Césaire indulge long in automatic writing when negritude was at stake.

Surrender to the heterogeneous, the complex, the contradictory does not suit every temperament. It requires an askesis of sorts, the grace of passivity. Picasso always claimed that painting was stronger than he was and made him do what it wanted.[29] From time to time, he would laugh at the numerous versions of the "painter painting" he put on canvas and joke, "And he thinks he's got it all worked out, the poor guy!"[30] Césaire (influenced in this respect by the traditional African relationship to plant life), makes the surrender a condition of rebirth. It is precisely this kind of *démarche* we find in the title poem of this collection, "Lost Body." Thematically, the poet giving up the so-called real world strives to eradicate his self ("more and more humble and more lowly"), fusing with vegetable life to the point that he falls into the tomb-womblike "live semolina of a well-opened earth" and experiences "DELICIOUS TOTAL ENCOUNTER," thus gaining knowledge ("I hiss yes I hiss very ancient things") and cosmogonic power ("with the insolent jet of my wounded and solemn shaft/I shall command the islands to be").

The parallels between "Lost Body" and Picasso's painting can be pursued even beyond the thematic aspects into the semantic. Césaire's use of nouns (even proper ones) as verbs ("I who Krakatoa . . . /I who Laelaps . . . /I omphale") amounts to the breaking down of grammatical categories, which is akin to Picasso's breaking down of the components of perspective. It also implies a sort of generalized and ongoing metamorphosis of the kind often found in Picasso's pieces (for example, *The Crane, Woman with a Pram, Woman with a Dog*, and so on), the multiple states of the object alluding to some essential common denominator. Moreover, the noun-verb confusion cancels the barrier between the acting subject and the action, between the I and the world, between art and life, a process characteristic not only of Picasso specifically but of modernism in general. Various scenes come to mind: Picasso covering a canvas with green because (he said) he had an indigestion from green and had to vomit it; Jarry living Pataphysics unto death; Rousseau trying to interest the Mexican ambassador in Paris in one of his "Mexican" paintings!

Last but not least, in its stongly consonantal beginning, *Lost Body* has the immediate physical impact of an African tom tom beat and dance—still a different statement on the part of Césaire. His frequent percussive effects (among them three poems called "Tom-Tom") were meant to weaken the resistance of the intellect (he boasted, however optimistically, that simple people often understood his poetry better than sophisticated ones) and to dislodge the diction from a Eurocentric position by creating a hybrid prosody in which the phonemic possibilities of French had been stretched to "a rupestral design in the stuff of sound."[31] So, to end our parallel, *Lost Body* relates to the sounds of more conventional French poetry not unlike the way in which the quasi-African mask faces of the *Demoiselles d'Avignon* relate to Western European painting.

❖   ❖   ❖

Thus both Picasso's art and Césaire's poetry succeed in putting the reader/viewer (voyeur?) in a central position from which—and only from which—the poem/painting can be truly born. No longer the recipient of a meaning already there, the reader/viewer's mind becomes the locus of significations. Between pure subjectivity (which can be identified with fetishism or magic) and the pure objectivity of bourgeois realism, Picasso and Césaire offer a third option in which the human mind and the world of objects embrace each other harmoniously. In painting it took a Catalan in perpetual exodus to achieve this; in poetry a man who by his very background, by his praxis, and by his esthetics symbolizes the formidable option represented by the emergence, between the Old World and the New

World, of a Third World both very old and very new. He said it himself: "The poet is that very ancient yet new being who... between absence and presence, searches for and receives in the sudden triggering of inner cataclysms, the password of connivance and power."[32]

The engravings date from March 1949. In June of that year, Picasso surrounded the title of each poem with an aquatint. The frontispiece to the volume, a superb profile of a black man wearing a wreath, the *poeta laureatus*, was engraved in Vallauris that December. The face looks boldly to the right—that is, to the inside of the book, the inner world, so to speak—and the strong, erect neck conveys pride in its blackness. The cover shows the title, *Corps Perdu*, inscribed in a vegetable-shaped heart.

Besides a frontispice, two engravings are provided for each poem. Their irregular distribution, the alternation of lithographs facing blank pages and of printed pages without corresponding pictures, the apparently capricious use or absence of frames around the images, suggest that in keeping with the tradition of the previous decades, this book posits the autonomy of illustrations in relation to text. However, the three themes in the engravings—vegetable, human, cosmic, the first two clearly influenced by Wifredo Lam's "magic realism"—respond to those of the poems.

The stylized vegetable forms (for instance, the second illustration in "Word," the first in "Elegy" and the last one in "Lay of Errantry") emphasize the pistil and the anthers, showing the flower in explosion, ejecting its fertilizing pollen, an image frequent in Césaire's poetry (for instance, "Were there/only one flying seed dreaming very loudly/that is enough" in "A Blank to Fill on the Travel Pass of the Pollen"). Several of these, half-vegetable and half-human, allude to the role of the "plant man" in Césaire's mythology as a symbol of the identification of the blacks with telluric values, among them nonaggressive growth, endurance, strength and serenity.

Among human figures, the frontispiece of "Word" connects with the "Cretan" vein in Picasso, characteristic of the ceramics he made

xxiii

at Vallauris over the next several years. Most of the others, however, are either hybrid (incorporating plant forms) or resemble prehistoric cave drawings, such as the striking shamanesque figure that serves as frontispiece to the poem "Lost Body." The large enigmatic face in the third illustration to the same poem is also reminiscent of Lam's visionary totemism in the voodoo tradition. Both face and figure remind one of the connections of the sacred with the beginnings of art, and both fit the magic ceremonial tone of the corresponding poem. The frontispieces of "Presence" and "Lay of Errantry" present interesting contrasts with the diametric content of the two poems. The former fills the page with a texture of elongated creatures exuding solidity, while the latter suggests the black "diaspora" by the scattering of violent motion and off-balance figures all over the page.

The erotic theme is conveyed sometimes by the frank and innocent sensuality of ambiguous vegetable elements (as in the first illustration of "Presence"), sometimes by male/female combinations ranging from abstract minimal curves (second lithograph in "Elegy"), to the stylized sun-and-moon motif (second lithograph in "Summons"), thus playing with the distance within the couple. As a bizarre variation on this motif, the second lithograph in "Forloining," a lyrical plantlike design, suggests the abuse of an abandoned, bent-over, long-haired female figure by a male figure (perhaps brandishing some cutting weapon) and depicts as eloquently as the poem does the ambiguous and quasi-ritualistic link between the white victim and her black assailant.

The frontispiece of "Summons" is the only lithograph in the collection not related to the human or the vegetable. Its starlike organization around a stable center, whence signals radiate, forms a good complement to a text in which the poet, a self-appointed cosmic bard, sings of "the chancellery of fire/the chancellery of water" and toys demiurgically with space and time.

Annette Smith
Clayton Eshleman

Notes

(All translations ours, unless otherwise specified)

[1]Clayton Eshleman and Annette Smith, *The Collected Poetry of Aimé Césaire*, Berkeley: University of California Press, 1983.

[2]Although major studies of Césaire include both, the most detailed biography is Thomas A. Hale, *Aimé Césaire: A Bio-bibliography*, in *Africana Journal* V, 1 (1974), and the most complete bibliography is Hale, *Les Ecrits d'Aimé Césaire: Bibliographie commentée* (Montréal: Presses de l'Université de Montréal, 1978).

[3]First version in *Volontés* 20 (August 1939). Later published by Brentano (New York, 1947) with a preface by André Breton; *édition définitive* published by Présence africaine (Paris, 1956, 1960, 1971); published and translated many times outside France.

[4]Re-edited in facsimile by Jacqueline Leiner (Paris: J. M. Place, 1978, 2 vols.).

[5]Paris: Gallimard, 1946, 1961, 1970. *And the Dogs Were Silent* (*Et les Chiens se taisaient*), a "lyrical oratorio," was published separately in 1956 (Paris: Présence africaine).

[6]First edition, Paris: K éditeur. Re-edited under the same title (taken from the last line of Apollinaire's *Zone*), along with *Corps perdu*, as part of *Cadastre* (Paris: Seuil, 1961). Both collections had been revised in the interim.

[7]See the bibliographical history on pages xx and the critical analysis on pages xx of this introduction.

[8]Paris:, Presses Universitaires de France, 1948.

[9]Published by Présence africaine in 1955.

[10]Paris: Présence africaine, 1956.

[11]First edition, Paris: Seuil. Won the René Laporte literary prize. Some of the poems had appeared previously in *Présence africaine* between 1955 and 1959.

[12]Respectively published in Paris by Présence africaine in 1963, in *Théâtre 5*, 1967 (subsequently Seuil, 1967) and in *Théâtre 22*, 1969 (subsequently Seuil, 1975).

[13] Paris: Seuil.

[14] See, for instance, Le Discours antillais (Paris: Seuil, 1981). While acknowledging Césaire's central role in the negritude movement, Glissant is representative of a younger generation that asserts the right of the Antilles to constitute a specific culture, antonomous from Europe's and based on the very diversity of their languages and history.

[15] "A Salute to the Third World/for Leopold Sedar Senghor," in Eshleman and Smith, The Collected Poetry of Aimé Césaire.

[16] A recent Césaire colloquium (Aimé Césaire, ou l'Athanor d'un alchimiste, Paris, November 21–23, 1985), attended by participants from twenty-two nations, made it clear that North and South American intellectuals feel as deeply indebted to the poet as those from Africa, the Caribbean, and Europe.

[17] Vol. I (January 1942), pp. 51–52.

[18] Vol. II (February 1943), pp. 39–41.

[19] Vol. II (1945), pp. 247, 256, 259.

[20] "Les Cubistes et les Poètes," Mercure de France, September 16, 1912. We are indebted to the June–July 1982 issue of Europe, which under the title Cubisme et Littérature, focused on the intersection of literature and painting in the first half of the twentieth century and conveniently gathers a great deal of information on this subject.

[21] La Jeune Poésie française, Paris: Rouart, 1917, pp. 201–202.

[22] Oeuvres Complètes, Paris: Gallimard, Bibliothèque de la Pléiade, 1968, pp. 982–983.

[23] Helène Parmelin, Picasso le peintre et son modèle (Paris: Editions Cercle d'art), p. 151.

[24] This quote and the previous one from Pierre Dufour, Picasso, 1950-1968, trans. by R. Allen (Geneva: Skira, 1969), pp. 19, 121.

[25] Susanne Césaire, "Misère d'une poésie," Tropiques (January 1942), vol. I, p. 50.

[26] "To Uphold Poetry" ("Maintenir la Poésie"), Tropiques 8–9 (October 1943), vol. II, 8.

[27] "Wifredo Lam," in Noria, Eshleman-Smith, The Collected Poetry.

[28] "Poetry and Knowledge" ("Poésie et Connaissance") in *Tropiques* 12 (January 1945), vol. I, p. 162 (trans. by J. Arnold in *Sulfur* 5, 1982).

[29] See Dufour, *Picasso*, p. 14.

[30] Parmelin, *Picasso le peintre et son modèle*, p. 121.

[31] The phrase ("un dessin rupestre dans la matière sonore") is from "Poetry and Knowledge" (see note 28), p. 164.

[32] Ibid., p. 170.

◆　◆　◆

Publisher's Note

Since the publication of the Fragrance limited edition of Lost Body in 1950, Aimé Césaire has substantially revised some of the poems in the suite, as well as its order. He has also entirely omitted the poem "Longitude" and has changed the title of "Au large" to "De forlange" ("Forloining" in English). For the present edition of this work, therefore, the poems in the English language version admitted to the authorized complete works published in 1983 have been adopted. The French version of the poems appears at the end of this volume.

LOST BODY

WORD

Among me

from myself

to myself

outside any constellation

clenched in my hands only

the rare hiccup of an ultimate raving spasm

keep vibrating word

I will have luck outside the labyrinth

longer wider keep vibrating

in tighter and tighter waves

in a lasso to catch me

in a rope to hang me

and let me be nailed by all the arrows

and their bitterest curare

to the beautiful center-stake of very cool stars

vibrate

vibrate you very essence of the dark

in a wing in a throat from so much perishing

the word nigger

sprung fully armed from the howling

of a poisonous flower

the word nigger

all filthy with parasites

the word nigger

loaded with roaming bandits

with screaming mothers

crying children

the word nigger

a sizzling of flesh and horny matter

burning, acrid

the word nigger

like the sun bleeding from its claw

onto the sidewalk of clouds

the word nigger

like the last laugh calved by innocence

between the tiger's fangs

and as the word sun is

    a cracking of bullets

and the word night

    a ripping of taffeta

the word nigger

    dense, right?

from the thunder of a summer

    appropriated by

        incredulous liberties

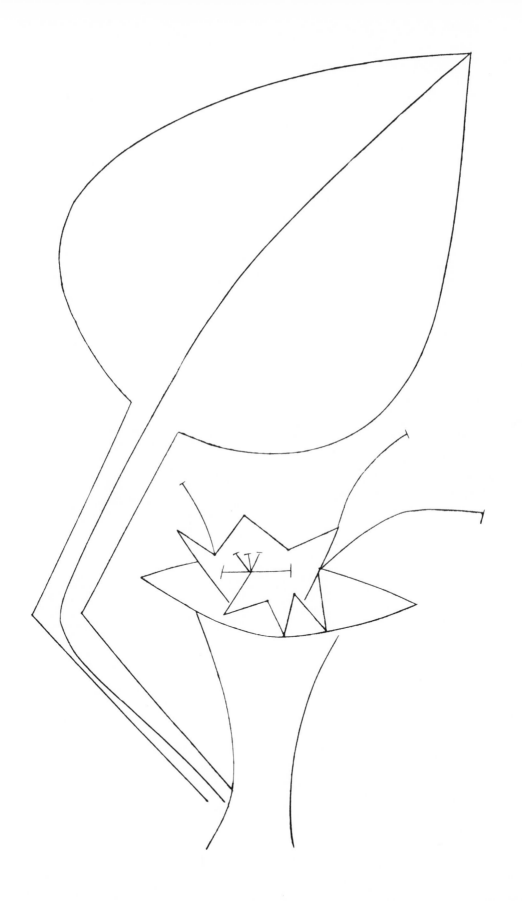

WHO THEN, WHO THEN . . .

And if I needed myself

needed a true sleep

blond as an awakening

a city escaping into the jungle or the sand

sniffed out nocturnal sniffed out

needed a nonritualistic god or you

or an era of millet and enterprise

and if I needed an island

Borneo Sumatra Maldives Laccadives

if I needed a sandalwood-scented Timor

or Moluccas Ternate Tidore

or Celebes or Ceylon

who in this vast magician night

would comb the ebb and the flow

with the teeth of a triumphant comb

and if I needed sun

or rain or blood

the cordial of an instant of an invented dawn

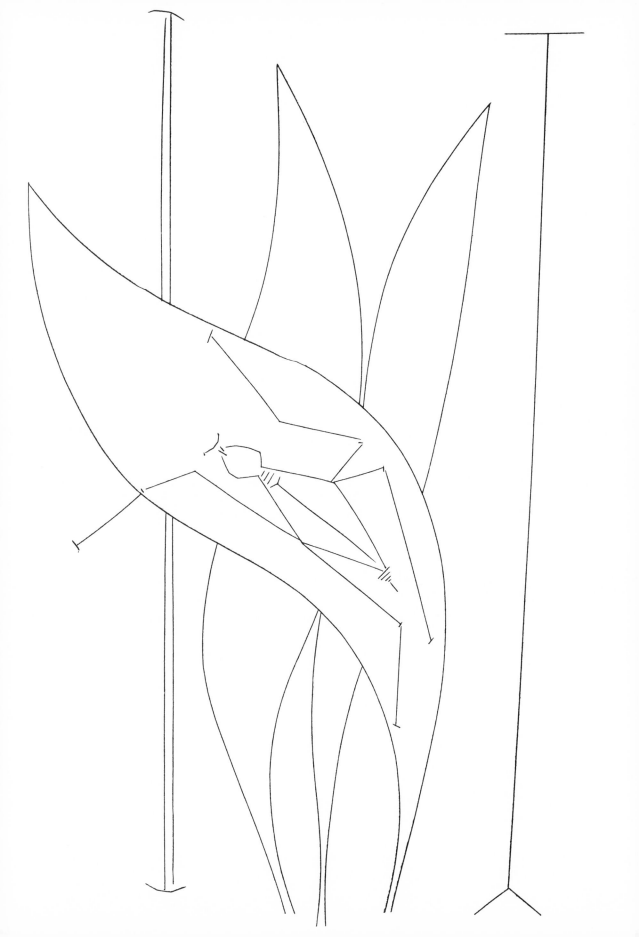

an unconfessed continent

a well a lizard a dream

an unstunted reverie

its memory pulmonic and

                    its heart in its hand

and if I needed a wave

        or a mizzen

or the grip phosphorescent

with an eternal scar

who then

who then

among the winds would comb

with a triumphant comb a vapor

        of changeable climates

who then

who then

O full-grown girl

      wild condemned to sort out

the grain of my shadow

from the grains of a clarity

who skillfully through dog-or-wolf dusk

      moves me forward

intent upon neatly

      confusing the accounts

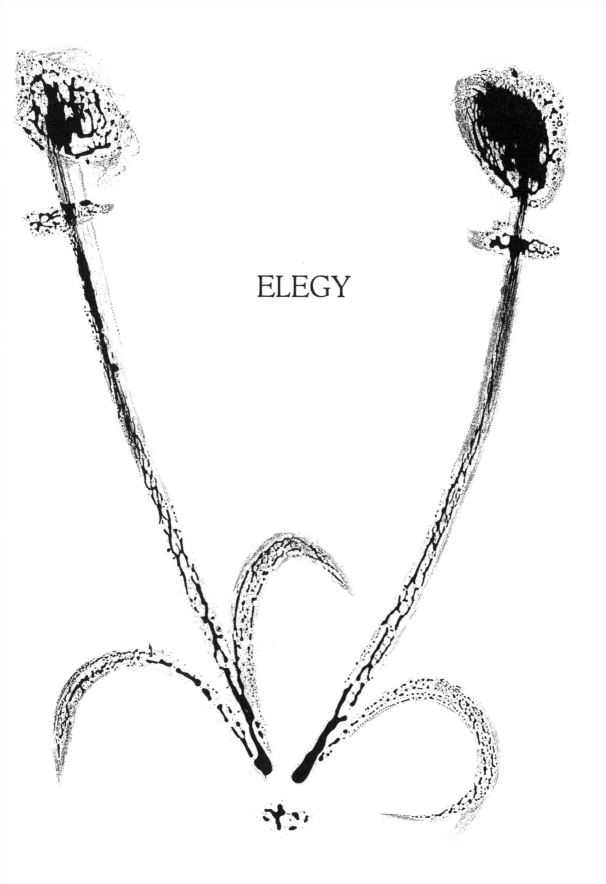

ELEGY

The hibiscus that is nothing other

than a burst eye

from which hangs the thread of a long gaze

the trumpets of the chalice vines

the huge black sabers of flamboyants

the twilight that is an ever jingling

bunch of keys

the Arecas that are nonchalant suns never setting

        because pierced through and through by a pin

          which the addlebrained lands

never hesitate to jab all the way in

to their hearts the terrifying souklyans Orion

the ecstatic butterfly that magical pollens

crucified on the gate of nights trembling

the beautiful black curls of cañafistulas

        that are very proud

mulatto women whose necks tremble a bit

        under the guillotine

and do not be surprised if at night

        I moan more heavily

or if my hands strangle more secretly

it is the herd of old sufferings

      which toward my smell

black and red

scolopendra-like

stretches its head

      and with the still soft and clumsy

insistence of its muzzle

searches more deeply for my heart

then it is no use for me

      to press my heart against yours

nor to lose myself

      in the foliage of your arms

the herd finds it

and very solemnly

in a manner always new

licks it

amorously

until the first blood savagely appears

on the abrupt open claws of

DISASTER

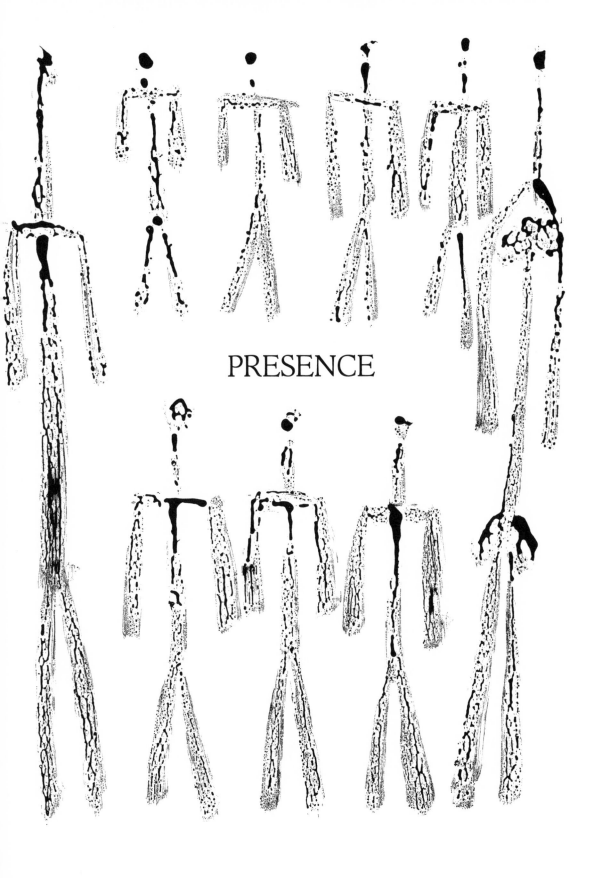

PRESENCE

a whole May of cañafistulas

on the chest of pure hiccup

of an island adulterous to its site

flesh which having possessed itself

harvests its grape self

O slow along the dacite

a pinch of birds fanned by a wind

in which the cataracts of time

        pass blended

the sheer profusion of a rare miracle

in the ever credulous storm

of a nonevasive season

FORLOINING

The houses out here

at the foot of the mountains

are not even as well arranged as hobnailed boots

the trees are explosions whose last spark

goes out washing over my hands

which tremble a little

from now on I carry within me

the sheath torn from a tall palm tree

like the day would be without the memory of you

the raw dodder silk

which ensnares the spine of the landscape

in the utterly complete way that despair does

monstrous solitary ceiba trees which

from this day on I would resemble

      stripped of the leaves of my love

I drift between a swell and swathes formed by

the speech tumult of albizzias

in front of me is an extraordinary peasant

what the peasant sings is a tale

about cane cutters

woosh the cane cutter

grabs the long-haired lady

hacks her into three pieces

woosh the cane cutter

buries not the maiden

he hacks her up in pieces

tosses them behind him

woosh the cane cutter

sings the peasant and proceeds

      without anger toward a cutlass evening

the disheveled hair of the long-haired lady

      makes rivulets of light

so sings the peasant

There are a whole lot of things
       whose names I do not know
and I'd like to tell you about them
in the sky your hair solemnly draws away
kinds of rain one no longer sees
nuts Saint Elmo's fire
suns lamés whispered nights
cathedrals too
which are the carcasses
       of large gnawed horses
spat by the sea from far away
but still worshipped by people
a whole lot of forgotten things
a whole lot of dreamed things

while the two of us

       Distant-one-my-inattentive-one

the two of us

enter the never faded landscape

more powerful than

       a hundred thousand ruttings

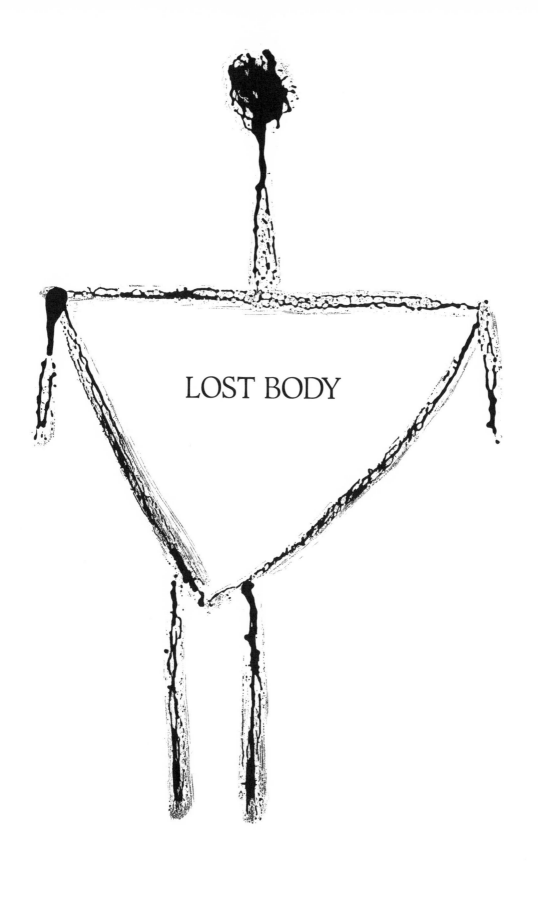

LOST BODY

I who Krakatoa

I who everything better than a monsoon

I who open chest

I who Laelaps

I who bleat better than a cloaca

I who outside the musical scale

I who Zambezi or frantic or rhombos or

       cannibal

I would like to be more and more humble

       and more lowly

always more serious

       without vertigo or vestige

to the point of losing myself falling

into the live semolina

       of a well-opened earth

Outside in lieu of atmosphere

       there'd be a beautiful haze no dirt in it

each drop of water forming a sun there

whose name the same for all things

would be DELICIOUS TOTAL ENCOUNTER

so that one would no longer know what goes by

—a star or a hope

or a petal from the flamboyant tree

or an underwater retreat

raced across by the flaming torches

      of aurelian jellyfish

Then I imagine life would flood

      my whole being

better still I would feel it

      touching me or biting me

lying down I would see

      the finally free odors come to me

like merciful hands

finding their way

to sway their long hair in me

longer than this past that I cannot reach.

Things stand back make room among you

room for my repose carrying in waves

my frightening crest of anchor-like roots

looking for a place to take hold

Things I probe I probe

me the street-porter I am root-porter

and I bear down and I force and I arcane

           I omphale

Ah who leads me back toward the harpoons

           I am very weak

I hiss yes I hiss very ancient things

as serpents do as do cavernous things

I whoa lie down wind

and against my unstable and fresh muzzle

against my eroded face

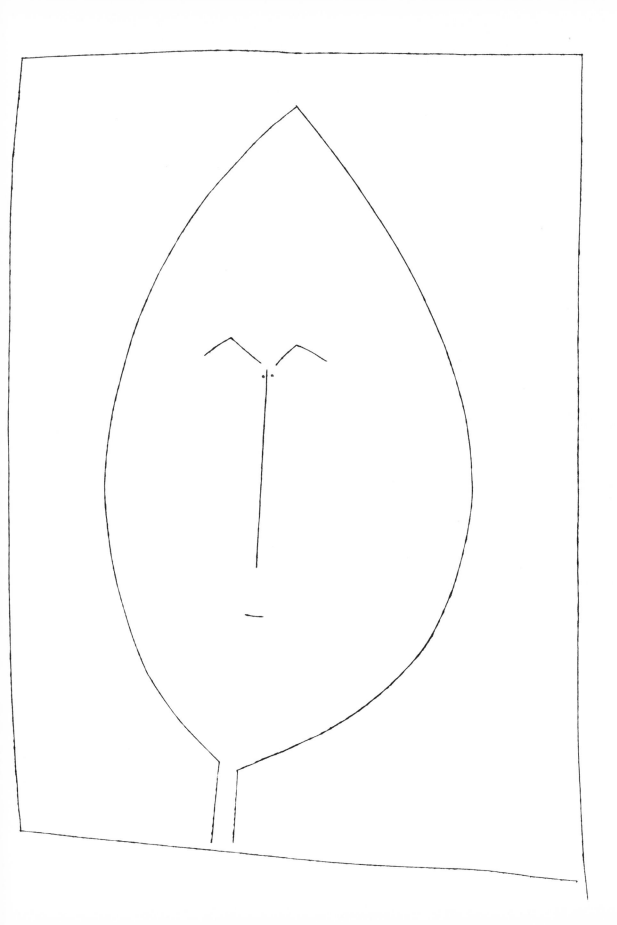

press your cold face of ravaged laughter

The wind alas I will continue to hear it

nigger nigger nigger from the depths

of the timeless sky

a little less loud than today

but still too loud

and this crazed howling of dogs and horses

which it thrusts at our forever fugitive heels

but I in turn in the air

shall rise a scream so violent

that I shall splatter the whole sky

and with my branches torn to shreds

and with the insolent jet

      of my wounded and solemn bole

       I shall command the islands to be

YOUR PORTRAIT

I say river corrosive

kiss of guts

river gash enormous embrace

in the smallest swamps

forced water frantic at the sluice gates

for with fresh tears

I built you into a river

poisonous

      spasmodic

         triumphant

which toward the flowering shores of the sea

tears open the slash of my manchineel course

I say river

like one says patient regal crocodile

quick to snap out of its dream

river

like royal anaconda

inventor of the sudden flick

river

jet alone like from the depths of nightmare

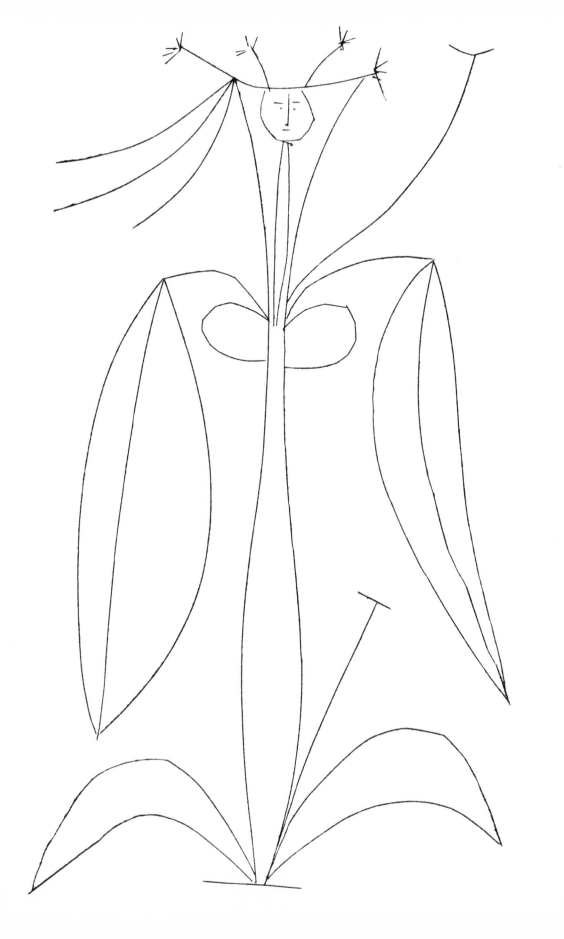

the baldest Peleé of mountains.

River

to which all is permitted

above all wash away my banks

widen me

that an ear I might auscultate

      the new coralline heart of the tides

and let the whole horizon venture forth

vaster and vaster before me

and take off from your snout

henceforth

      swirling

         and liquid

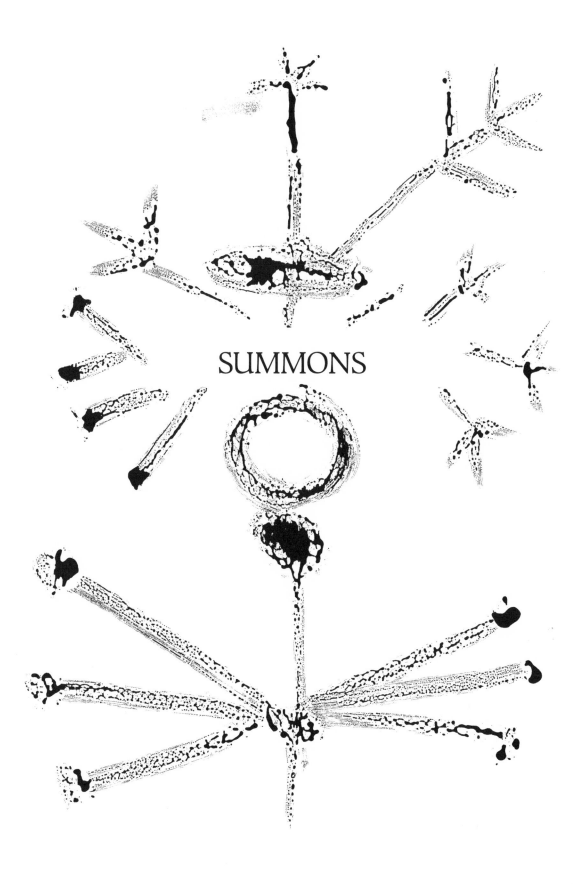

SUMMONS

everything more beautiful

the chancellery of fire
the chancellery of water

a huge somersault of promontories
and stars

a mountain exfoliating into

an orgy of islands into glowing trees

the coldly calm hands of the sun

over the wild head of

      a destroyed city

everything more beautiful

      everything more beautiful

including the memory

      of this world sweeping through

a warm white gallop fluffy with black

like that of a sea bird

      which forgets itself

         in full flight and glides

on pink legs over sleep

everything more beautiful

      truly more beautiful

umbel

and terebella

the chancellery of air

the chancellery of water

your eyes a fruit bursting

      its shell on the stroke of midnight

and it no longer is

      MIDNIGHT

Space conquered Time the conqueror

me I like time time is nocturnal

and when Space galloping sets me up

Time comes back to set me free

Time Time

oh creel without venison

      summoning me

whole

      native

           solemn

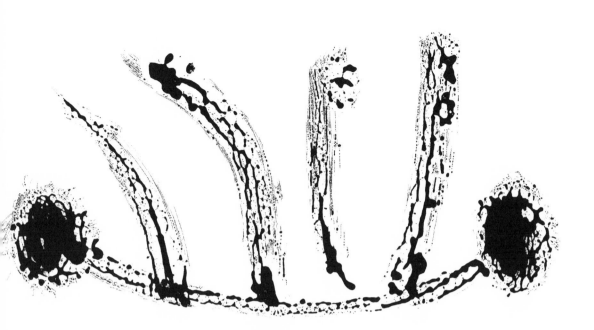

BIRTHS

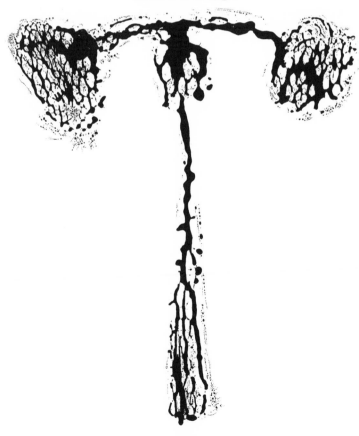

Broken

Stagnant water of my face

on our births broken at last

Let me say this:

in the stagnant waters of my face

alone

distant

nocturnal

never

never

will I have been absent

The serpents?

the serpents, we'll drive them away

The monsters?

The monsters—the remorse of all

the days we indulged in

biting us—will lower their breathing

sniffing us.

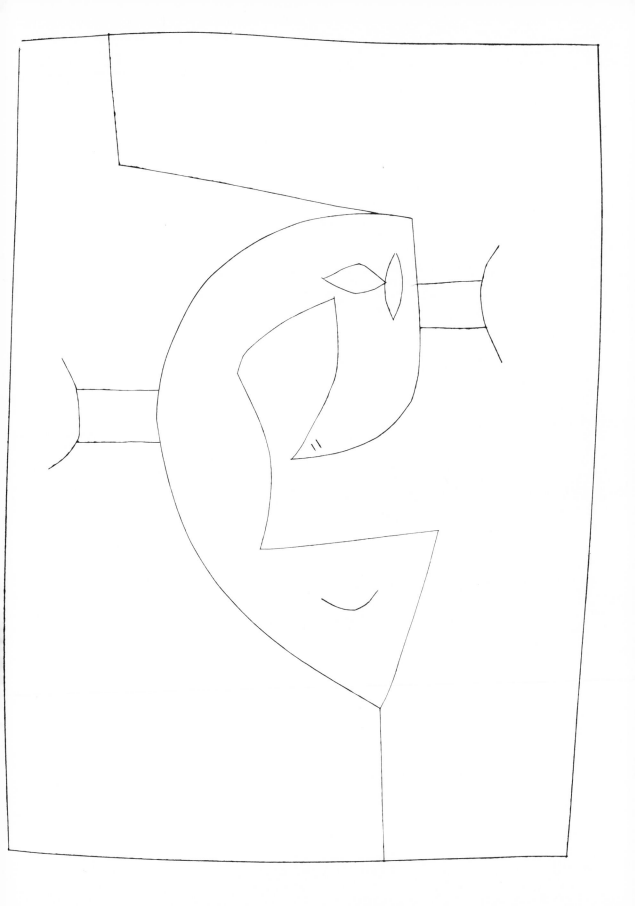

All the shed blood

we shall lap it up

from it we shall grow like spelt

with more exact dreams

with less divided thoughts

do not blow the dust away

the antivenom shall balance

      the antique venom in

           an awesome rose window

do not blow the dust away

everything shall be visible rhythm

and what would we recover?

not even our secret.

Do not blow the dust away

A wild unfaltering passion

     the source of all expansion

there shall be escarbuncles

     everywhere no less enchantment-

prone than the enchanted tree

nontree tree

yesterday uprooted

and behold

the celestial plowmen are proud

     having been transformed

oh plowing plowmen

on earth it is replanted

the sky thrusts

it counter-thrusts

nontree tree

beautiful voluminous tree

           day alights on it

           a startled bird

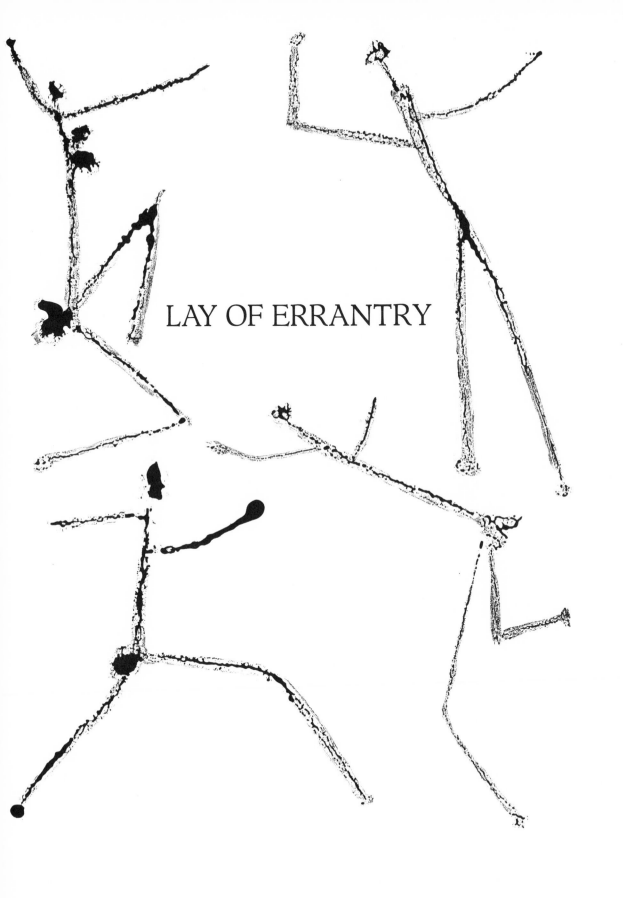

LAY OF ERRANTRY

Everything that was ever torn apart

has been torn apart in me

everything that was ever mutilated

has been mutilated in me

in the middle of the platter stripped of breath

the cut fruit of the moon forever on its way

toward the to-be-invented contour of its other side

and yet what remains with you of former times

little more perhaps than a certain urge

to prick up my ears or to tremble in the night rain

and whereas some sing the return of Christmas

to dream of stars

astray

this is the shortest day of the year

on command all has collapsed into all

the words the faces the dreams

even the air has become infected

when a hand reaches toward me

I barely infer its intention

I have this so lachrymose season well in mind

the day had a taste of childhood

of something deep something mucous

evilly turned toward the sun

iron against iron an empty station

where—no trains to be taken—

the same arm always moaning grew hoarse in vain

Exploded sky flayed curve

of flogged slaves' backs

grief treasurer of the trade winds

shut book of spells forgotten words

I question my mute past

Island of gore of gulfweed

island suction of a shark-sucker

island after-laugh of whales

island gist of a risen bubble

island great heart poured out

high most distant best hidden

drunk weary fisherwoman

      worked to death

drunk beautiful hand bird-snared

ill-joined island disjointed island

every island beckons

every island is a widow

Benin Benin oh embittered aggry

life which was once Uphaz

a mouth of the Zambezi

toward an Ophir with no Albuquerque

will we always stretch out our hands?

Long ago oh rended one

in bits and pieces She

gathered her dismembered one

and the fourteen pieces

took their triumphant place in the rays of evening

I invented a secret cult

my sun is the sun always awaited

the fairest of suns is the nocturnal sun

Woman's body restituted island

woman's body full freighted

woman's body foam-born

woman's body retrieved island

which is never carried away enough

oh ranunculated night

not to carry its polypary secret to the sky

woman's body palm tree gait

coifed by the sun with a nest

in which the phoenix dies and is reborn

we are souls of noble birth

nocturnal bodies lively with lineage

faithful trees spouting wine

I a flebile sibyl.

Inert waters of my childhoods

into which the oars barely sunk

myriad birds of my childhoods

where if ever was the fragrant island

illuminated by great suns

the season the setting so delicious

the year paved with precious stones?

Quartered in the perturbations

     of the zones

tenebrous mixture

     at the height of its cry

I saw a male bird founder

the stone is embedded in his forehead

I contemplate the lowest point of the year

Filth-stained body skillfully shed

space wind of deceitful trust

space false planetary pride

slow rough diamond-cutter prince

might I be the sport of negromancy?

Now more skillful than Antilia or Brazil

a milestone in the distance

the sword of a flame that racks me

I fell the trees of Paradise

CORPS PERDU

French Text

◆ MOT

Parmi moi
de moi-même
à moi-même
hors toute constellation
en mes mains serré seulement
le rare hoquet d'un ultime spasme délirant
vibre mot

j'aurai chance hors du labyrinthe
plus long plus large vibre
en ondes de plus en plus serrées
en lasso où me prendre
en corde où me pendre
et que me clouent toutes les flèches
et leur curare le plus amer
au beau poteau-mitan des très fraîches étoiles

vibre
vibre essence même de l'ombre
en aile en gosier c'est à force de périr
le mot nègre
sorti tout armé du hurlement
d'une fleur vénéneuse
le mot nègre
tout pouacre de parasites
le mot nègre

tout plein de brigands qui rôdent

des mères qui crient
d'enfants qui pleurent
le mot nègre
un grésillement de chairs qui brûlent
âcre et de corne
le mot nègre
comme le soleil qui saigne de la griffe
sur le trottoir des nuages
le mot nègre
comme le dernier rire vêlé de l'innocence
entre les crocs du tigre
et comme le mot soleil est un claquement de balles
et comme le mot nuit un taffetas qu'on déchire
le mot nègre
        dru savez-vous
du tonnerre d'un été
   que s'arrogent
       des libertés incrédules

◆ QUI DONC, QUI DONC . . .

    Et si j'avais besoin de moi
d'un vrai sommeil
blond de même qu'un éveil
d'une ville s'évadant dans la jungle ou le sable

flairée nocturne flairée
d'un dieu hors rite ou de toi
d'un temps de mil et d'entreprise

et si j'avais besoin d'une île
Bornéo Sumatra Maldives Laquedives
si j'avais besoin d'un Timor parfumé de sandal
ou de Moluques Ternate Tidor
ou de Célèbes ou de Ceylan
qui dans la vaste nuit magicienne
aux dents d'un peigne triomphant
peignerait le flux et le reflux

et si j'avais besoin de soleil
ou de pluie ou de sang
cordial d'une minute d'un petit jour inventé
d'un continent inavoué
d'un puits d'un lézard d'un rêve
songe non rabougri
la mémoire poumonneuse et le cœur dans la main
et si j'avais besoin de vague ou de misaine
ou de la poigne phosphorescente
d'une cicatrice éternelle
qui donc
qui donc
aux vents d'un peigne triomphant
peignerait une fumée de climats inconstants

qui donc
qui donc
O grande fille à trier sauvage condamnée
en grain mon ombre
des grains d'une clarté
et qui savamment entre loup et chien m'avance
attentif à bien brouiller les comptes

◆ELEGIE

L'hibiscus qui n'est pas autre chose qu'un œil éclaté
d'où pend le fil d'un long regard les trompettes des solandres
le grand sabre noir des flamboyants le crépuscule
          qui est un trousseau de clefs toujours sonnant
les aréquiers qui sont de nonchalants soleils jamais couchés
          parce qu'outrepercés d'une épingle que les
               terres à cervelle brûlée
n'hésitent jamais à se fourrer
jusqu'au cœur les souklyans effrayants Orion
l'extatique papillon que les pollens magiques
crucifièrent sur la porte des nuits tremblantes
les belles boucles noires des canéfices qui sont des mulâtresses
trés fiéres dont le cou tremble un peu sous la guillotine

et ne t'étonne pas si la nuit je geins plus lourdement
ou si mes mains étranglent plus sourdement
c'est le troupeau des vieilles peines qui vers mon odeur

noir et rouge

en scolopendre

allonge la tête et d'une instance du museau

encore molle et maladroite

cherche plus profond mon cœur

alors rien ne me sert de serrer mon cœur contre le tien

et de me perdre dans le feuillage de tes bras

il le trouve

et très gravement

de maniére toujours nouvelle

le léche

amoureusement

jusqu'à l'apparition sauvage du premier sang

aux brusques griffes ouvertes du

DESASTRE

♦ PRESENCE

tout un mai de canéficiers

sur la poitrine de pur hoquet

d'une île adultère de site

chair qui soi prise de soi-même vendange

O lente entre les dacites

pincée d'oiseaux qu'attise un vent

où passent fondues les chutes du temps

la pur foison d'un rare miracle
dans l'orage toujours crédule
d'une saison non évasive

◆ DE FORLONGE

Les maisons de par ici au bas des montagnes
ne sont pas aussi bien rangées que des godillots
les arbres sont des explosions dont la derniére étincelle
vient écumer sur mes mains qui tremblent un peu
désormais je porte en moi
la gaine arrachée d'un long palmier
comme serait le jour sans ton souvenir
la soie grège des cuscutes
qui au piège prennent le dos du site
de la manière très complète du désespoir
des ceibas monstrueux seuls auxquels
dès maintenant je ressemblerais dépouillé
        des feuilles de mon amour
je divague entre houle et javelles que fait tumultueuse
la parole des albizzias
il y a en face de moi un paysan extraordinaire
ce que chante le paysan c'est une histoire
de coupeur de cannes

han le coupeur de cannes
saisit la dame à grands cheveux

en trois morceaux la coupe

han le coupeur de cannes
la vierge point n'enterre
la coupe en morceaux

les jette derriére
han le coupeur de cannes

chante le paysan et vers un soir
      de coutelas s'avance sans colère
les cheveux décoiffés de la dame aux grands
      cheveux font des ruisseaux de lumière
ainsi chante le paysan
Il y a des tas de choses dont je ne sais pas le nom
et que je voudrais te dire
au ciel ta chevelure qui se retire solennellement
des pluies comme on n'en voit jamais plus des noix
des feux Saint-Elme
des soleils lamés des nuits murmurées
des cathédrales aussi
qui sont des carcasses de grands chevaux rongés
que la mer a crachés de très loin
mais que les gens continuent d'adorer
des tas de choses oubliées
des tas de choses rêvées
tandis que nous deux Lointaine-ma-distraite
nous deux

120

dans le paysage nous entrons jamais fané
plus forts que cent mille ruts

◆ CORPS PERDU

       Moi qui Krakatoa
moi qui tout mieux que mousson
moi qui poitrine ouverte
moi qui laïlape
moi qui bêle mieux que cloaque
moi qui hors de gamme
moi qui Zambèze ou frénétique ou rhombe ou cannibale
je voudrais être de plus en plus humble et plus bas
toujours plus grave sans vertige ni vestige
jusqu'à me perdre tomber
dans la vivante semoule d'une terre bien ouverte.
Dehors une belle brume au lieu
       d'atmosphère serait point sale
chaque goutte d'eau y faisant un soleil
dont le nom le même pour toutes choses
serait RENCONTRE BIEN TOTALE
si bien que l'on ne saurait plus qui passe
ou d'une étoile ou d'un espoir
ou d'un pétale de l'arbre flamboyant
ou d'une retraite sous-marine
courue par les flambeaux des méduses-aurélies
Alors la vie j'imagine me baignerait tout entier

mieux je la sentirais qui me palpe ou me mord
couché je verrais venir à moi les odeurs enfin libres
comme des mains secourables
qui se feraient passage en moi
pour y balancer de longs cheveux
plus longs que ce passé que je ne peux atteindre.
Choses écartez-vous faites place entre vous
place à mon repos qui porte en vague
ma terrible crête de racines ancreuses
qui cherchent où se prendre
Choses je sonde je sonde
moi le porte-faix je suis porte-racines
et je pèse et je force et j'arcane
       j'omphale
Ah qui vers les harpons me raméne
       je suis très faible
je siffle oui je siffle des choses très anciennes
de serpents de choses caverneuses
Je or vent paix-là
et contre mon museau instable et frais
pose contre ma face érodée
ta froide face de rire défait.
Le vent hélas je l'entendrai encore
nègre nègre nègre depuis le fond
du ciel immémorial
un peu moins fort qu'aujourd'hui
mais trop fort cependant
et ce fou hurlement de chiens et de chevaux

qu'il pousse à notre poursuite toujours marronne
mais à mon tour dans l'air
je me léverai un cri et si violent
que tout entier j'éclabousserai le ciel
et par mes branches déchiquetées
et par le jet insolent de mon fût blessé et solennel

je commanderai aux îles d'exister

◆ TON PORTRAIT

je dis fleuve corrosif
baiser d'entrailles
fleuve entaille énorme étreinte
dans les moindres marais
eau forcée forcenant aux vertelles
car avec les larmes neuves
je t'ai construite en fleuve
vénéneux
                    saccadé
                            triomphant
qui vers les rives en fleur de la mer
lance en balafre ma route mancenilliére

Je dis fleuve
comme qui dirait patient crocodile royal
prompt à sortir du rêve

fleuve
comme anaconda royal
l'inventeur du sursaut
fleuve
jet seul comme du fond du cauchemar
les montagnes les plus Pelées.
Fleuve
à qui tout est permis
surtout emporte mes rives
élargis-moi
à ausculter oreille le nouveau cœur corallien des marées
et que tout l'horizon de plus en plus vaste
devant moi
et à partir de ton groin s'aventure
désormais
       remous
          et liquide

◆ SOMMATION

toute chose plus belle

la chancellerie du feu
la chancellerie de l'eau

une grande culbute de promontoires
et d'étoiles

124

une montagne qui se délite en
orgie d'îles en arbres chaleureux
les mains froidement calmes du soleil
sur la tête sauvage d'une ville détruite

toute chose plus belle toute chose plus belle
et jusqu'au souvenir de ce monde y passe
un tiède blanc galop ouaté de noir
comme d'un oiseau marin qui s'est oublié
          en plein vol et glisse
sur le sommeil de ses pattes roses

toute chose plus belle en vérité plus belle
ombelle
et térébelle
la chancellerie de l'air
la chancellerie de l'eau
tes yeux un fruit qui brise sa coque sur le coup de minuit
et il n'est plus MINUIT

l'Espace vaincu le Temps vainqueur
moi j'aime le temps le temps est nocturne
et quand l'Espace galope qui me livre
le Temps revient qui me délivre
le Temps le Temps
ô claie sans venaison qui m'appelle

intègre
natal
solennel

◆ NAISSANCES

Rompue
Eau stagnante de ma face
sur nos naissances enfin rompues
C'est entendu
dans les stagnantes eaux de ma face
seul
distant
nocturne
jamais
jamais
je n'aurai été absent.

Les serpents?
les serpents, nous les chasserons
Les monstres?
Les monstres—nous mordant
les remords de tous les jours
où nous ne nous complûmes—baisseront le souffle
nous flairant.

126

Tout le sang répandu
nous le lécherons
en épeautres nous en croitrons
de rêves plus exacts
de pensées moins rameusès
ne soufflez pas les poussiéres
l'anti-venin en rosace terrible équilibrera l'antique venin

ne soufflez pas les poussiéres
tout sera rythme visible
et que reprendrions-nous?
pas même notre secret.
Ne soufflez pas les poussiéres
Une folle passion toujours roide étant
   ce par quoi tout sera étendu
ce seront plus que tout escarboucles émerveillables
pas moins que l'arbre émerveillé
arbre non arbre
hier renversé

et vois
les laboureurs célestes sont fiers d'avoir changé
ô laboureurs laboureurants
en terre il est replanté
le ciel pousse
il contre-pousse

arbre non arbre
bel arbre immense
                    le jour dessus se pose
                    oiseau effarouché

◆DIT D'ERRANCE

            Tout ce qui jamais fut déchiré
en moi s'est déchiré
tout ce qui jamais fut mutilé
en moi s'est mutilé
au milieu de l'assiette de son souffle dénudé
le fruit coupé de la lune toujours en allée
vers le contour à inventer de l'autre moitié

et pourtant que te reste-t-il du temps ancien

        à peine peut-être certain sens
dans la pluie de la nuit de chauvir ou trembler
            et quand d'aucuns chantent Noël revenu
            de songer aux astres
            égarés

voici le jour le plus court de l'année
ordre assigné tout est du tout déchu
les paroles les visages les songes
l'air lui-même s'est envenimé

128

quand une main vers moi s'avance
j'en ramène à peine l'idée
j'ai bien en tête la saison si lacrimeuse
le jour avait un goût d'enfance
de chose profonde de muqueuse
vers le soleil mal tourné
fer contre fer une gare vide
où pour prendre rien
s'enrouait à vide à toujours geindre le même bras

Ciel éclaté courbe écorchée
de dos d'esclaves fustigés
peine trésorière des alizés
grimoire fermé mots oubliés
j'interroge mon passé muet

Ile de sang de sargasses
île morsure de remora
île arrière-rire des cétacés
île fin mot de bulle montée
île grand cœur déversé
haute la plus lointaine la mieux cachée
ivre lasse pêcheuse exténuée
ivre belle main oiselée
île maljointe île disjointe
toute île appelle
toute île est veuve
Bénin Bénin ô pierre d'aigris

Ifé qui fut Ouphas
une embouchure de Zambèze
vers une Ophir sans Albuquerque
tendrons-nous toujours les bras?

jadis ô déchiré
Elle pièce par morceau
rassembla son dépecé
et les quatorze morceaux
s'assirent triomphants dans les rayons du soir

J'ai inventé un culte secret
mon soleil est celui que toujours on attend
le plus beau des soleils est le soleil nocturne

Corps féminin île retournée
corps féminin bien nolisé
corps féminin écume-né
corps féminin île retrouvée
et qui jamais assez ne s'emporte
qu'au ciel il n'emporte
ô nuit renonculée
un secret de polypier
corps féminin marche de palmier
par le soleil d'un nid coiffé
où le phénix meurt et renaît
nous sommes âmes de bon parage
corps nocturnes vifs de lignage

arbres fidèles vin jaillissant
moi sybille flébilant.

Eaux figées de mes enfances
où les avirons à peine s'enfoncèrent
millions d'oiseaux de mes enfances
où fut jamais l'île parfumée
de grands soleils illuminée
la saison l'aire tant délicieuse
l'année pavée de pierres précieuses?

Aux crises des zones écartelé
en plein cri mélange ténébreux
j'ai vu un oiseau mâle sombrer
la pierre dans son front s'est fichée
je regarde le plus bas de l'année

Corps souillé d'ordure savamment mué
espace vent de foi mentie
espace faux orgueil planétaire

lent rustique prince diamantaire
serais-je jouet de nigromance?
Or mieux qu'Antilia ni que Brazil
pierre milliaire dans la distance
épée d'une flamme qui me bourrelle
j'abats les arbres du Paradis

LOST BODY

◆ ◆ ◆

The design of Lost Body is based on Corps Perdu designed by Pablo Picasso and published by Editions Fragrance (Paris, 1950) in a limited edition of 219 copies. Picasso chose to set Aimé Césaire's poems in Erasmus, designed by S. H. de Roos, a medeival-style type dating from 1923 with light serifs, tall ascenders, short descenders, and an unusual lower-case g. A new typeface, Vermeer, has been designed by AlphaOmega especially for this edition of Lost Body, with digital composition by ASD Typesetting Service of Poughkeepsie, New York, using High Technology Solutions, Multi-language Publishing System. Vermeer is based on Erasmus' proportions and feel, but has a more contemporary appearance.

Lost Body has been designed by Cynthia Hollandsworth
and printed on Mohawk Vellum cream. Printing and
binding by Murray Printing Company
of Westford, Massachusetts.